THE
GREAT
PHILOSOPHERS

Consulting Editors
Ray Monk and Frederic Raphael

Richard Webster

FREUD

Weidenfeld & Nicolson
LONDON

First published in Great Britain in 2003
by Weidenfeld & Nicolson

A CIP catalogue record for this book
is available from the British Library.

ISBN 0 297 82985 8

Typeset by Deltatype Ltd, Birkenhead, Merseyside

Printed in Great Britain by Clays Ltd, St Ives plc

Weidenfeld & Nicolson

The Orion Publishing Group Ltd
Orion House
5 Upper Saint Martin's Lane
London, WC2H 9EA

ACKNOWLEDGEMENTS

I am particularly grateful to Professor Frank Cioffi and to Allen Esterson for their comments on a draft version of this book.

FREUD

FREUD AND PSYCHOLOGY

Of all the thinkers who, in the last two hundred years, have shaped our understanding of human nature, there can be no doubt that Sigmund Freud is one of the most important. Indeed, if we were to walk through a hall of fame in which the statues of well-known thinkers were displayed on a scale which corresponded to their perceived cultural greatness and their general acclaim, Freud's monument would tower over practically every other. In the entire history of Western thought perhaps only Plato and Marx would loom on anything approaching the same scale. And in this imaginary hall of fame many of the heroes of professional philosophy, from Spinoza and Kant to Hume, would be represented by statues so small as to be virtually invisible.

What gives Freud this towering pre-eminence, a pre-eminence which he seems to maintain even in the face of the fiercest and best-armed of his critics? One way of answering this question is to consider the extent and nature of the transformation which he brought about in the discipline of psychology.

Before the advent of Darwin, psychology, like the natural sciences in general, was deeply rooted in religion. Just as physicists such as Isaac Newton, himself a devout Christian, scrutinised nature in an attempt to unlock the secrets of its divine creator, so those who studied human nature were driven by similar religious imperatives. Indeed psychology had originally been but a branch of Christian theology, the word having been created in the fifteenth century by theologians engaged in the study of the soul. In common with many other forms of modern scholarship, the secular discipline of psychology, which gradually emerged during the nineteenth century, retained many assumptions and habits of mind which belonged to an age of faith. It had its roots on the one hand in the thought of Plato and on the other in the teachings of Jesus and Paul. What the Platonic and the Christian traditions had in common was the belief that human beings are made up of two separate entities: an animal body which was created by God, and a mind, spirit or soul which was given by God uniquely to Man.

Traditionally psychology was concerned not with the study of the impure animal body of human beings but with their rational soul. The mentalism of psychology and its particular interest in cognitive phenomena – such as memory, intelligence and perception – is a heritage of this soul-centred perspective. By creating psychoanalysis at the end of the nineteenth century, however, Freud challenged the traditional outlook. A discipline which had previously been concerned with a selected, relatively pure extract of human existence, suddenly seemed to deal with the whole of human life. The deepest feelings of ordinary men and women, and above all their sexual impulses, which Plato had explicitly excluded from philosophy as a form of intellectual pollution, and which later philosophers had tended to avoid, were now apparently located at the very heart of the new science of psychoanalysis.

In 1917 the Harvard biologist William Morton Wheeler, having written disparagingly of academic psychologies which 'ignore or merely hint at the existence of such stupendous and fundamental biological phenomena as hunger, sex and fear', went on to welcome the work of psychoanalysts who 'have had the courage to dig up the subconscious, that hotbed of all the egotism, greed, lust, pugnacity, cowardice, sloth, hate and envy which every single one of us carries about as his inheritance from the animal world'.[1]

The enormous appeal of any form of psychology which claims to deal fearlessly with one of the most fascinating of all subjects – our animal inheritance and above all the nature of human sexual desire, and the variety of human sexual behaviour – should not be underestimated. It is perhaps partly because of this appeal that many have not hesitated to hail Freud as a true intellectual revolutionary – as the Darwin of the mind. In order to assess whether Freud merits this title, and whether his achievement justifies the towering pre-eminence he continues to enjoy in our culture, it is necessary to relate how psychoanalysis came into being, and why it was that Freud came to place sex at the very centre of the science he created.

HYSTERIA, ANNA O. AND THE INVENTION
OF PSYCHOANALYSIS

Sigmund Freud was born in 1856, in the small Austro-Hungarian town of Freiberg. Unusually he was born in a caul – a kind of membrane – and his mother immediately took this as a portent of his future fame. She called him *'mein goldener Sigi'*, and throughout his childhood and early adolescence in Vienna he was surrounded by his parents' adulation and by their urgent expectation of his future greatness. As Freud embarked on a career in medicine, which eventually led him to study in the newly emerging field of neurology, these expectations seem to have become increasingly burdensome. For, although outwardly successful, he appears to have begun to despair of ever being granted the kind of world-redeeming revelation which he felt inwardly compelled to seek.

Freud's earliest unsuccessful skirmish with fame took place in 1885 when, after experimenting with taking cocaine, he sought medical glory by publishing a paper on the drug as a miracle-therapy. In writing this paper, however, he failed to observe the crucial properties of the drug as a local anaesthetic while simultaneously omitting to warn against cocaine addiction. Freud, however, was not deterred by this unfortunate episode from seeking medical distinction. He almost immediately left Vienna for Paris where, from October 1885 to February 1886, he studied under the famous neurologist Charcot.

Charcot specialised in treating patients who were suffering from a variety of unexplained physical symptoms including paralysis, contractures (muscles which contract and cannot be relaxed) and seizures. Some of these patients sporadically and compulsively adopted a bizarre posture (called *arc-de-cercle*) in which they lay down and arched their body backwards until they were supported only by their head and their heels. Charcot eventually came to the conclusion that many of his patients were suffering from a form of hysteria which had been induced by their emotional response to a traumatic accident in their past – such as a fall from a scaffold or a railway crash. They suffered, in his view, not from the physical effects of the accident, but from the idea they had formed of it.

Freud was immensely impressed by Charcot's work on traumatic hysteria and took from it the notion that one of the principal forms of neurosis came about when a traumatic experience led to a process of unconscious symptom-formation. He now began to develop this idea, and did so partly by reference to the work of a medical colleague, Josef Breuer. Freud was especially interested in the most unusual of all his colleague's patients, the celebrated 'Anna O.' whom Breuer had begun to treat in 1880.

Anna O. was a twenty-one-year-old woman who had fallen ill while nursing her father who eventually died of a tubercular abscess. Her illness began with a severe cough. She subsequently developed a number of other physical symptoms, including paralysis of the extremities of the right side of her body, contractures and disturbances of vision, hearing and language. She also began to experience lapses of consciousness and hallucinations.

Breuer diagnosed Anna O.'s illness as a case of hysteria

and gradually developed a form of therapy which he believed was effective in relieving her symptoms. He came to the conclusion that when he could induce her to relate to him during the evening the content of her daytime hallucinations, she became calm and tranquil. Breuer saw this as a way of 'disposing' of the 'products' of Anna O.'s 'bad self' and understood it as a process of emotional catharsis. The patient herself described it as 'chimney sweeping', and as her 'talking cure'.

Breuer went on to extend this therapy. At one point in her illness, for a period of weeks, Anna O. declined to drink and would quench her thirst with fruit and melons. One evening, in a state of self-induced hypnosis, she described an occasion when she said she had been disgusted by the sight of a dog drinking out of a glass. Soon after this she asked for a drink and then woke from her hypnosis with a glass at her lips.

In his published account of the case, written some twelve years later, Breuer treated the story which Anna O. had related in a trance as a true account of an incident which had given rise to her aversion to drinking. He said he had concluded that the way to cure a particular symptom of 'hysteria' was to recreate the memory of the incident which had originally led to it and bring about emotional catharsis by inducing the patient to express any feeling associated with it.

The sudden disappearance of one of Anna O.'s many symptoms thus became the basis for what Breuer later described as a 'therapeutic technical procedure'. According to both Freud and Breuer, this method had been applied systematically to each of Anna's symptoms and as a result she was cured completely of her hysteria.

The case of Anna O. played a fundamental role in the development of Freud's thought. She has frequently been described as the first psychoanalytic patient, a view which Freud himself, lecturing at Clark University in the United States, once endorsed:

> If it is a merit to have brought psychoanalysis into being, that merit is not mine. I had no share in its earliest beginnings. I was a student and working for my final examinations at the time when another Viennese physician, Dr Josef Breuer, first (in 1880–2) made use of this procedure on a girl who was suffering from hysteria.[2]

Freud, however, was understating his own role. Psychoanalysis would never have come into being if he had not transformed Breuer's 'talking cure' by marrying it with Charcot's views on traumatic hysteria and his own elaborate technique for reconstructing repressed memories through interpretation and free-association.

The patients whom Freud endeavoured to psychoanalyse at this early stage of his career almost all resembled Anna O. in at least one respect: they came to Freud not because they were experiencing emotional distress but because they were suffering from *physical* symptoms. Freud's first patient, for example, Frau Emmy von N., suffered speech difficulties, which Freud described as 'spastic interruptions amounting to a stammer'. She was also plagued 'by frequent convulsive *tic*-like movements of her face and the muscles of her neck' and was compulsively given to making repetitive verbal exclamations and clicking sounds. Another patient, Lucy R., an English governess, suffered from strange olfactory hallucinations centering on the smell of burnt pudding. Yet another, Elisabeth von R., came to Freud because she had been suffering for more than two years from pains in her legs.

In all these cases Freud construed his patients' illness as hysteria and set about uncovering the traumatic incident which had supposedly given rise to their symptoms. In order to help the process of analysis he developed what he called his 'pressure technique'. This consisted in applying pressure to his patients' foreheads with his hands and instructing them to report faithfully 'whatever appeared before their inner eye or passed through their memory at the moment of pressure'. Freud rapidly developed such faith in the effectiveness of this method for evoking pictures, ideas or unconscious 'memories' that he came to regard it as infallible, maintaining that if no images or memories were produced by the first application of pressure, repeated pressure would invariably be effective. When, in the course of treating Elisabeth von R. for her lameness, he suspected her of concealing thoughts from him, he decided to reinforce the physical pressure with mental pressure:

I no longer accepted her declaration that nothing had occurred to her, but assured her that something *must* have occurred to her. Perhaps, I said, she had not been sufficiently attentive, in which case I would be glad to repeat my pressure. Or perhaps she thought that her idea was not the right one. This, I told her, was not her affair; she was under an obligation to remain completely objective and say what had come into her head, whether it was appropriate or not. Finally I declared that I knew very well that something *had* occurred to her and that she was concealing it from me; but she would never be free of her pains so long as she concealed anything. By thus insisting I brought it about that from that time forward my pressure on her head never failed in its effect.[3]

At this period Freud believed that, in the final stages of therapy, it was helpful 'if we can guess the ways in which things are connected up and tell the patient before we have uncovered it'.[4] When, however, he presented Elisabeth von R. with his conclusion, namely that her illness had been precipitated by her falling in love with her brother-in-law, she objected that this was not true. Freud, however, persisted in his explanation and eventually reported that his patient had been cured.

FREUD AND SEX

Freud and Breuer initially appeared to be at one in their understanding of hysteria and in the therapeutic approach they recommended to it. In 1895 they set out their theory in detail in a jointly authored book, *Studies on*

Hysteria. In the introduction, amidst frequent acknowledgements of Charcot's influence, they suggested that the hidden memory of a psychical trauma 'acts like a foreign body which long after its entry must continue to be regarded as an agent that is still at work'. As evidence for this they cited the therapeutic procedure which Breuer had devised:

> For we found, to our great surprise at first, that *each individual hysterical symptom immediately and permanently disappeared when we had succeeded in bringing clearly to light the memory of the event by which it was provoked and in arousing its accompanying affect, and when the patient had described that event in the greatest possible detail and had put the affect into words* [italics in original].[5]

'Hysterics,' they continued, 'suffer mainly from reminiscences.' To this celebrated formulation they might have added that the physical symptoms of such patients are formed out of *repressed* reminiscences which they are unable, without therapeutic help, to retrieve as memories.

If psychoanalysis began as a joint enterprise between Breuer and Freud, however, Freud gradually developed it in a direction which led to a rift with Breuer. The reason for this rift was sex. In particular it was the centrality Freud accorded to sexuality in the medical theories he now developed about hysteria and its origins.

One of the sources of Freud's interest in sex as a causative factor in disease may well have been Charcot himself, the teacher Freud revered above all others. He would eventually

12

recall an evening reception in 1886, at which he had overheard Charcot arguing that a particular young woman owed her medical problems to her husband's inadequate sexual performance:

> Charcot suddenly broke out with great animation: '*Mais dans des cas pareils c'est toujours la chose génitale, toujours, toujours, toujours*' [But in cases like this it's always the genital thing – always, always, always]: and he crossed his arms over his stomach, hugging himself and jumping up and down on his toes several times in his own characteristically lively way.

By 1888 Freud was already suggesting that 'conditions relating functionally to sexual life play a great part in the aetiology of hysteria.'[6]

In fact both Breuer and Freud were led towards sexual experiences as a potential cause of hysteria. Where Freud differed from Breuer was in his determination to treat sexual factors as the *sole* source of hysteria. In doing this he was influenced by his admiration for the germ theory of disease which had been put forward by Koch and Pasteur. What this novel theory implied was that all genuine diseases had a single cause and that one of the main purposes of medical research was to discover the micro-organism or other agent which was responsible for it. If hysteria was a genuine disease, as Freud, following Charcot, believed it to be, then it must be caused by a single pathogen. In Freud's view the pathogen in question was a sexual one.

If there were medical reasons for Freud's decision to

locate sex at the centre of psychoanalysis, however, it would seem that there were also psychological reasons. Freud once observed that 'mankind has always harboured the longing to open all secrets with a single key'.[7] He himself appears to have been particularly driven by such a need and it was his insistence on a single sexual explanation of hysteria which eventually led to the split with Breuer. 'Freud,' Breuer would write in 1907, 'is a man given to absolute and exclusive formulations: this is a psychical need which, in my opinion, leads to excessive generalization.'

THE SEDUCTION THEORY

The most important of Freud's sexual theories at this time focused on the possibility that memories of sexual abuse in early childhood might be repressed, and that this repression might give rise to physical symptoms. 'Just think,' he wrote to his friend, the Berlin physician Wilhelm Fliess, in October 1895, 'among other things I am on the scent of the following strict precondition for hysteria, namely, that a primary sexual experience (before puberty), accompanied by revulsion and fright must have taken place . . .' A week later Freud wrote to Fliess again. The idea which he had initially presented as a conjecture, and which has since become known as 'the seduction theory', had by this point become a 'secret' which Freud imparted to his friend in a state of evident intellectual excitement:

> Have I revealed the great clinical secret to you, either
> orally or in writing? Hysteria is the consequence of a
> presexual *sexual shock*... 'Presexual' means actually
> before puberty, before the release of sexual substances;
> the relevant events become effective only as memories.[8]

Although it is frequently assumed that Freud arrived at this
conclusion on the basis of his patients' recollections, this
was not the case. Derived as it was from the model of
unconscious symptom-formation he had adapted from
Charcot, the theory maintained that a sexual trauma
experienced in childhood would *only* have a pathogenic
effect if the supposed victim had no conscious memory of
it.

The purpose of Freud's therapeutic sessions at this stage
of his career was therefore not to listen to his patients'
spontaneous recollections of sexual abuse. It was, as in the
Anna O. case, to reconstruct scenes of which they had no
recollection, and then to encourage patients to give vent to
feelings of fear or disgust they had not expressed at the
time. As he wrote in his paper 'The Aetiology of Hysteria':

> Before they come for analysis the patients know nothing
> about these scenes. They are indignant as a rule if we
> warn them that such scenes are going to emerge. Only
> the strongest compulsion of the treatment can induce
> them to embark on a reproduction of them ... even
> after they have gone through them once more in such a
> convincing manner, they still attempt to withhold belief
> from them, by emphasising the fact that, unlike what

happens in the case of other forgotten material, they have no feeling of remembering the scenes.[9]

At this point in his career, in the crucial years 1896–7 (when he was still using his 'pressure technique'), it is evident that Freud knew exactly the kind of scenes he expected to uncover and that the process of treatment could only end when such a scene was produced: 'If the first-discovered scene is unsatisfactory, we tell our patient that this experience explains nothing, but that behind it there must be hidden a more significant, earlier experience ... A continuation of the analysis then leads in every instance to the reproduction of new scenes of the character we expect.'[10]

Freud himself evidently played an active role in constructing these scenes. One example of the ingenuity with which he did so is provided by the case of a young woman who came to him suffering both from a speech impediment and from eczema which had led to lesions in the corner of her mouth. Freud's questioning of the woman, and his interpretation of her answers, led him to the conclusion that her speech inhibition had first appeared when 'with a full mouth she was fleeing from a woman teacher'. Noting that her father had similarly explosive speech 'as though his mouth were full' and referring to a similar case which had involved fellatio, Freud presented his patient with the conclusion that both her cracked mouth and her speech impediment were hysterical symptoms caused by her father forcing her to suck his penis when she had been a child.

The woman initially accepted this explanation, but after

speaking to her father she became convinced of his innocence. Freud, however, remained confident that his analysis was correct and construed his patient's outward resistance to it as a sign of her inner acceptance: 'I have threatened to send her away and in the process convinced myself that she has already gained a good deal of certainty [about her father's guilt] which she is reluctant to acknowledge.'[11]

Freud believed that some cases went back to infancy. 'The early period before the age of 1½ years is becoming ever more significant,' he wrote to Fliess on 24 January 1897. 'Thus I was able to trace back, with certainty, a hysteria that developed ... for the first time at eleven months and [I could] hear again the words that were exchanged between two adults at that time! It is as though it comes from a phonograph.'[12]

Although his colleagues were sceptical, and although the distinguished sexologist, Krafft-Ebing, characterised the seduction theory as a 'scientific fairy tale', Freud insisted that it rested on sound evidence:

Only the most laborious and detailed investigations have converted me, and that slowly enough, to the view I hold today. If you submit my assertion that the aetiology of hysteria lies in sexual life to the strictest examination, you will find that it is supported by the fact that in some eighteen cases of hysteria, I have been able to discover this connection in every single symptom, and, where circumstances allowed, to confirm it by therapeutic success.[13]

Privately, however, he began to have doubts. In September 1897 he confided to his friend Fliess that he no longer believed in his seduction theory. He now admitted that he had not in fact been able to bring a single case to a conclusion, that some of his patients had 'run away', and that his partial successes, where particular symptoms had disappeared during the treatment, could be explained in other ways.

Freud's seduction theory did not belong simply to a passing phase in his intellectual development, for he spent some two years under its spell, reconstructing episodes in his patients' lives which he construed as confirming it, and seeking to win over his medical colleagues. He had expended all this energy for the very simple reason that he evidently believed he had at last been given the theoretical revelation which he sought. In 'The Aetiology of Hysteria' he offered a public estimate of the importance of his new theory, actually claiming to have discovered 'the source of the Nile' in the field of neuropathology. Privately he saw it as bringing the fulfilment of the dreams of fame he had entertained almost constantly for the previous ten years: 'The expectation of eternal fame was so beautiful,' he wrote to Fliess, 'as was that of certain wealth, complete independence, travels, and lifting the children above the severe worries that robbed me of my youth.'[14]

Given the depth of his commitment to the seduction theory it is perhaps not surprising that eight years were to pass before he was able to admit in public that parts of the theory were in need of revision. Only much later, in 1914, did he acknowledge that the theory had actually been mistaken.

In practice it would appear that he was unable to discard his original sexual theory even in private until he had begun to construct the new theory which would replace it. One of the reasons why the discarded theory remains so important to any understanding of Freud's thought is that his new sexual theory would be poured into the mould formed by the old one. Although Freud abandoned the idea of childhood seduction as the sole cause of neurosis, he remained committed to the belief that neurotic illness had its roots in early childhood, that sexuality was the pathogenic factor, and that his technique for reconstructing repressed memories was essentially sound.

INFANTILE SEXUALITY

By this point in his career, Freud had virtually severed his links with the original 'discoverer' of psychoanalysis, Josef Breuer. The new mentor on whom he increasingly relied for theoretical inspiration was Wilhelm Fliess. Fliess was a nose and throat specialist who practised in Berlin. In 1887 he had travelled to Vienna to undertake postgraduate studies and, at the suggestion of Breuer, he attended some of Freud's neurology lectures. The two physicians had a great deal in common. Both were Jewish, both had studied under Charcot and both were given to large-scale theory-building.

Fliess had a particular interest in the relationship he believed to exist between the nose and the vagina. His monograph on this subject, *The Relations between the Nose and the Female Sexual Organs from the Biological Aspect*, was published in 1897. In this he set out a theory of periodicity whereby the two periods of 28 and 23 days, which he derived from the menstrual cycle, contained within them a key by which the mysteries of all biology might be unlocked. This key could be obtained by performing various arithmetical calculations using not only the figures 23 and 28 themselves but also their sum (51) and their difference (5). He eventually came to accord equal significance to the squares and cubes of these numbers, to their product and to other arithmetical transformations of them. Through such calculations, he maintained, organic life could be related to the motions of the stars, for 'the wonderful exactitude with which the period of 23 or 28 whole days is maintained allows one to presume a profound relationship between astronomical conditions and the creation of organisms.'[15]

Freud was immensely impressed by his friend's idea, describing it as 'a fundamental biological discovery'. He repeatedly urged Fliess to enlarge the scope of his theories and once wrote that he had set his hopes on him solving a particular problem 'as on the Messiah'. In one of the most significant letters he ever wrote, he looked forward with mystical ecstasy to a meeting at which Fliess would impart to him a new aspect of his doctrine: 'At Aussee I know a wonderful wood full of ferns and mushrooms, where you shall reveal to me the secrets of the world of lower animals and the world of children.'[16]

When Freud spoke of these 'secrets' he was referring to Fliess's application of contemporary Darwinian biology to child-psychology – to Fliess's theory of infantile sexuality. This theory was based on the idea that the human foetus in the womb, in developing from a unicellular organism, through fish-like and mammalian stages, to a fully formed human being, was re-enacting evolutionary history. As Ernst Haeckel, Darwin's foremost German disciple, put it, 'the embryonic development is an epitome – a condensed and abbreviated recapitulation – of the historical development of the species.' Haeckel, however, took things further than this common observation. He believed that all organisms possessed souls and that the soul, or consciousness, depended for its development on external stimuli. For this reason he maintained that while the body recapitulated the entire history of evolution in the womb, the soul remained 'in a state of embryonic slumber, a state of repose which Preyer has justly compared to the hibernation of animals'.[17]

The implication of this was that the newly born baby possessed, within a completely evolved body, a soul which was only partly evolved. The young child would then recapitulate at the level of consciousness or mental life the same stages of animal evolutionary development which had already been recapitulated physically inside the womb. This idea, if it was true, had clear implications for the development of human sexuality. For according to contemporary evolutionary theory as expounded by another German thinker, Wilhelm Bölsche, the line of evolutionary development was one in which simple organisms used the mouth as a reproductive organ, sexual reproduction being originally 'a sort of higher eating'. In more complex organisms such oral reproduction was displaced by the cloacal intercourse practised by reptiles and birds and described by Bölsche as 'anus pressed against anus'. This form of copulation was in turn displaced among crocodiles by the penis and vagina. If this line of evolutionary development was recapitulated in humans then every child would, in the first years of its life, pass through these same stages according to a biologically predetermined sequence. Each stage of 'perverse', animal sexuality would eventually succumb to automatic *organic* repression. The child would gradually progress from having the sexual consciousness of a simple animal to having that of a reptile. The oral and anal stages of sexuality would then be left behind as the child gradually achieved a fully human sexual consciousness.

Freud did not, of course, express his theory of infantile sexuality in these precise terms. But it was this view, which appears to have reached him initially through Fliess, that he eventually adopted. In his *Three Essays on the Theory of Sexuality*, which appeared in 1905, and in subsequent writings, Freud suggested that the sexual instinct was already present in newly born children and that it passed through three main stages – the oral, the anal and the phallic. Sexual pleasure was first experienced in relation to the mouth:

If an infant could speak, he would no doubt pronounce

the act of sucking at his mother's breast by far the most important in his life. He is not far wrong in this, for in this single act he is satisfying at once the two great vital needs . . . Sucking at the mother's breast is the starting-point of the whole of sexual life, the unmatched prototype of every later sexual satisfaction, to which phantasy often enough recurs in times of need. This sucking involves making the mother's breast the first object of the sexual instinct.[18]

In the next stage of development, the anal stage, Freud suggested that the pleasurable stimulation of the mucous membrane of the mouth ceded primacy to the same kind of stimulation of the anus:

We conclude that infants have feelings of pleasure in the process of evacuating urine and faeces and that they soon contrive to arrange those actions in such a way as to bring them the greatest possible yield of pleasure through the corresponding excitations of the erotogenic zones of the mucous membrane.

At this point, according to Freud, the child encountered for the first time external hostility to its quest for pleasure:

An infant must not produce his excreta at whatever moment he chooses, but when other people decide that he shall. In order to induce him to forego these sources of pleasure, he is told that everything that has to do with these functions is improper and must be kept secret. This is where he is first obliged to exchange pleasure for social respectability. From the outset his [own] attitude to his excreta themselves is quite different. He feels no disgust at his faeces, values them as a portion of his own body with which he will not readily part, and makes use of them as his first 'gift'.[19]

According to Freud, children obtained sexual pleasure by means which were predominantly 'auto-erotic': they stimulated their own erotogenic zones through sensual sucking, through excretion or through genital masturbation. Only at a later stage of development would the child's libido (sexual energy) become organised under the primacy of the genitals, and be subordinated to the purpose of sexual reproduction.

The normal course of human sexual development was, in Freud's view, biologically predetermined by 'phylogeny', which is to say the evolutionary history of the species:

The order in which the various instinctual impulses come into activity seems to be phylogenetically determined; so, too, does the length of time during which they are able to manifest themselves before they succumb to the effects of some freshly emerging instinctual impulse or to some typical repression. Variations, however, seem to occur both in temporal sequence and in duration, and these variations must exercise a determining influence upon the final result.[20]

With the formulation of this theory Freud had effectively brought into being a new form of childhood sexuality from which neurotic illness might be derived. A failure on the part of any individual to progress normally through this sequence – either because of some external traumatic event or because of some internal developmental anomaly – might result in sexual 'perversion' or neurosis. The individual would then become fixated at stages of 'sexual consciousness' which belonged phylogenetically to reptiles or other early forms of animal life, and this fixation would manifest itself in forms of sexual behaviour which Freud sometimes described as 'archaic'. 'Among animals,' wrote Freud, 'one can find, so to speak, in petrified form, every species of perversion of the [human] sexual organisation.'[21]

Freud's theory of infantile sexuality, which he began tentatively to construct even before he privately abandoned his 'seduction theory', became progressively more complex as the years went by. It would eventually entirely replace his ideas about childhood sexual seduction. It would provide, in effect, the new theoretical theatre in which Freud's original therapeutic drama could be acted out once again, this time with spectacular success. Before this could happen, however, at least one more theoretical innovation had to be made.

THE OEDIPUS COMPLEX

In late 1897, as if in an attempt to free himself from his recently abandoned seduction theory, Freud embarked on a process of self-analysis in which, by examining his dreams and memories, he sought to explore his own unconscious. In doing so, writes his biographer, Ernest

Jones, he was 'following a path hitherto untrodden by any human being'. It is generally held that it was during the course of this heroic self-analysis that Freud was able to retrieve memories of the sexual desire he had felt for his mother on an occasion when, as a young child, he had seen her naked. It was these memories which had led him to the discovery of the Oedipus complex.

The reality of what happened is quite different. Freud's formulation of the Oedipus complex had come about, as had so many of his theories, as a result of a suggestion made to him by his friend Fliess. This is evident from the terms in which Freud himself reported his discovery to Fliess. Freud wrote that, between the age of two and two and a half, 'my libido towards *matrem* was awakened, namely on the occasion of a journey with her from Leipzig to Vienna, during which we must have spent the night together and there must have been an opportunity of seeing her *nudam* (you inferred the consequences of this for your son long ago as a remark revealed to me). . .' From this passage it is clear that Freud had not in fact remembered seeing his mother naked. Nor had he recalled being sexually aroused. He had remembered only a long train journey from whose duration he *deduced* that he might have seen his mother undressing. His further speculation that he was sexually excited as a result is derived, as he himself notes, from something which Fliess had already told him. He is referring, it would appear, to Fliess's report that his son Robert had an erection (at a much younger age), supposedly as a result of seeing his mother naked.[22]

Less than two weeks after he had reported this artificially reconstructed memory to Fliess, Freud used it as the basis for a psychological law: 'I have found in my own case too [the phenomenon of] being in love with my mother and jealous of my father, and I now consider it a universal event in early childhood.' Freud went on to refer to 'the gripping power' of *Oedipus Rex*, suggesting that at the heart of the drama was a compulsion which everyone recognises. 'Everyone in the audience was once a budding Oedipus in fantasy and each recoils in horror from the dream fulfilment here transplanted into reality. . .'[23]

In formulating the Oedipus complex Freud was not referring to any general attraction felt by young boys for their mothers. He was referring specifically to a sexual impulse which supposedly emerges during the phallic phase of sexual development, and which leads to the young boy desiring to possess his mother genitally:

When a boy (from the age of two or three) has entered the phallic phase of his libidinal development, is feeling pleasurable sensations in his sexual organ and has learnt to procure these at will by manual stimulation, he becomes his mother's lover. He wishes to possess her physically in such ways as he has divined from his observations and intuitions about sexual life, and he tries to seduce her by showing her the male organ which he is proud to own. In a word his early awakened masculinity seeks to take his father's place with her. . . His father now becomes a rival who stands in his way and whom he would like to get rid of.[24]

According to Freud, the boy's desire to sexually possess his mother will eventually be met with the threat of castration. In the face of this horrifying threat, the boy abandons his sexual designs upon his mother, identifies with the father, and eventually seeks sexual satisfaction from other women.

Although the claims which Freud made for his new theory were initially modest, they gradually became larger and larger until he wrote that 'if psychoanalysis could boast of no other achievement than the discovery of the repressed Oedipus complex, that alone would give it a claim to be included among the precious new acquisitions of mankind.'[25]

Freud eventually placed the Oedipus complex at the very centre of the theory of infantile sexuality. So multifarious were the pathological consequences of failing to pass through the Oedipal stage smoothly, that it could be regarded as another universal pathogen. 'The Oedipus complex,' Freud wrote, 'may justly be regarded as the nucleus of the neuroses.'[26] Indeed, by treating it in this way Freud eventually came to the realisation that he could effectively rescue his seduction theory from the ignominy which otherwise threatened it. For he could present the seduction scenes he had reconstructed not as part of a disastrous error, but as the unrecognised precipitates of incestuous fantasising on the part of his patients. It was this view which he advanced in 1925 in his 'Autobiographical Study':

> It could not be disputed that I had arrived at these scenes by a technical method which I considered

correct, and that their subject-matter was unquestionably related to the symptoms from which my investigation had started. When I had pulled myself together, I
was able to draw the right conclusions from my
discovery: namely that the neurotic symptoms were not
related directly to actual events but to wishful fantasies,
and that as far as the neurosis was concerned psychical
reality was of more importance than material reality. I do
not believe even now that I forced the seduction
fantasies on my patients, that I 'suggested' them. I had
in fact stumbled for the first time upon the *Oedipus
complex*, which was later to assume such an overwhelm-
ing importance, but which I did not recognise as yet in
its disguise of fantasy.[27]

According to this view, the theory which Krafft-Ebing had
dismissed as 'a scientific fairy tale', and which Freud himself
had abandoned as mistaken, could now be recognised for
what it was – a brilliant though flawed intimation of the
greatest of all the discoveries of psychoanalysis.

DORA

A number of the cases Freud conducted after he had
begun to formulate the Oedipus complex closely
resembled his earliest attempts at psychoanalysis. One of
the most striking features of these early cases – that the
patients who came to Freud generally complained of

physical symptoms – is also found in the celebrated case of Dora.

Dora was an attractive eighteen-year-old young woman who had suffered at one point from severe bouts of coughing. She subsequently succumbed to a feverish illness which was diagnosed as appendicitis. At the same time she had begun to drag her right foot. Not long afterwards she seemed to become suicidal and also suffered a convulsive seizure during which she lost consciousness. She had also had catarrh and stomach troubles. It was at this stage that Freud began to treat her.

Freud had no hesitation in deciding that this was another case of hysteria. He then concluded that Dora's spasmodic cough, 'which, as is usual, was referred for its exciting stimulus to a tickling in her throat', was actually a somatic representation of a scene she had imagined in which Herr K., a friend of her father's who had made a sexual advance to her, engaged in an act of oral sex with his wife. In his account of the case Freud writes that a short time after Dora had 'tacitly' accepted this explanation, her cough vanished. He adds that he does not wish to lay too much stress on this since her cough had often disappeared spontaneously.

At a later stage in the analysis, however, Freud reached the conclusion that although Dora had rejected Herr K.'s advance with disgust, she was really in love with him. He went on, as was his custom, to inform his patient of his view:

> My expectations were by no means disappointed when
> this explanation of mine was met by Dora with a most

emphatic negative. The 'No' uttered by a patient after a repressed thought has been presented to his conscious perception for the first time, does no more than register the existence of a repression and its severity; it acts, as it were, as a gauge of the repression's strength. If this 'No', instead of being regarded as the expression of an impartial judgment (of which, indeed, the patient is incapable), is ignored, and if work is continued, the first evidence soon begins to appear that in such a case 'No' signifies the desired 'Yes'.[28]

Freud, in other words, is able to convince himself that when Dora says 'no', her very vehemence indicates that she really wants to say 'yes'. He subsequently decides that his patient is suffering from the effects of masturbation, and claims that her catarrh confirms this. Following Fliess, who believed that masturbation gave rise to enuresis, Freud forces Dora to confess that she had been a bed-wetter. When he puts pressure on her to solve the enigma of her illness 'by confessing that she had masturbated, probably in childhood', Dora is unable to comply, saying that she can remember no such thing. A few days later, however, Freud notices that she is fingering her reticule and immediately construes this as a 'step towards the confession':

Dora's reticule, which came apart at the top in the usual way, was nothing but a representation of the genitals, and her playing with it, her opening it and putting her finger in it, was an entirely unembarrassed yet unmistakable pantomimic announcement of what she would like to do with them – namely, to masturbate.[29]

Although Freud's conclusion that Dora had masturbated in childhood is based purely on ill-informed medical conjecture, and on a speculative interpretation of a common form of fidgeting, he now proceeds to talk about 'the occurrence of masturbation in Dora's case' as something which has been 'verified'.

Freud's analysis of Dora eventually ended when Dora ran away – or at least failed to return to resume her treatment. Freud was clearly hurt by the sudden ending of his therapeutic relationship with this attractive young woman. But he remained philosophical. 'No one,' he wrote, 'who like me, conjures up the most evil of those half-tamed demons that inhabit the human breast, and seeks to wrestle with them, can expect to come through the struggle unscathed.'[30]

THE WOLF MAN

Dora had first come to Freud in 1900 and his account of the case appeared in 1905. As psychoanalysis developed, however, Freud began to see more patients who came to him because of emotional disturbances rather than physical symptoms.

One such patient was the Russian nobleman Serge Pankejeff, who is generally known as the Wolf Man, the subject of one of Freud's most famous case histories. Although his initial debilitating illness was a severe gonorrhoeal infection, he subsequently became depressed and had been diagnosed as suffering from manic depressive insanity. He came to Freud in 1910 and his analysis lasted more than four years.

In his case history Freud places great emphasis on a dream the patient remembered having as a four-year-old boy. The patient had recalled that in his dream he was lying in his bed when the window suddenly opened of its own accord and he saw with terror six or seven white wolves sitting on the walnut tree in the garden. The wolves were quite white and had big tails like foxes; they were very still and were looking at him intently. Terrified of being eaten, he had woken up and screamed.

According to Freud's intricate analysis, conducted over a period of years, the dream was a disguised version of a traumatic primal scene. The six or seven wolves represent the boy's two parents, the difference in numbers being brought about by the unconscious in an attempt to disguise the dream's true meaning. The stillness of the wolves is an inverted reference to violent motion of the kind that would occur in sexual intercourse. The whiteness of the animals signifies the whiteness of the parents' underclothes. The wolves' staring at the boy is another inversion which actually signifies the boy staring at his parents. The bigness of their tails signifies, in the same upside-down manner, a tail which has been docked – an idea which in turn relates to the boy's fear of castration.

These and other interpretive strategies eventually enable Freud to claim that the dream was really a disguised memory of an occasion when, at the age of eighteen months, the young Serge had woken from his sleep one hot summer afternoon in the same room where his parents had retired, half-undressed, for a siesta. The boy had then witnessed his father having sexual intercourse with his mother from behind, three times in succession.

In advancing this interpretation of the dream, Freud believed he had uncovered the primal traumatic incident which had led directly to his patient's illness. However, he found that the patient was making no perceptible progress. In an attempt to break down his patient's 'resistance', he therefore set a date for the treatment to finish. It was after this, according to the case history he subsequently wrote, that, four years into the analysis, 'there emerged, timidly and indistinctly, a kind of recollection that at a very early age ... he must have had a nursery-maid who was very fond of him.' Freud writes that the name of this nursery maid was Grusha and that on one occasion, when he was two years old, Serge had seen her cleaning the floor. He had then urinated and she had threatened him with castration. In Freud's view the significance of this scene was as follows:

> When he saw the girl on the floor engaged in scrubbing it, and kneeling down, with her buttocks projecting and her back horizontal, he was faced once again with the posture which his mother had assumed in the copulation scene. She became his mother to him: he was seized with sexual excitement ... and, like his father (whose action he can only have regarded at the time as micturition), he behaved in a masculine way to her. His micturition on the floor was in reality an attempt at

seduction, and the girl replied to it with a threat of castration, just as though she had understood what he meant.[31]

It would appear from the case history that not long after he had reconstructed this quasi-Oedipal scene, his patient recovered. For Freud reports that the deadline he set for his patient worked, and that 'in a disproportionately short time the analysis produced all the material which made it possible to clear up [the patient's] inhibitions and remove his symptoms.'[32]

ANNA FREUD

If psychoanalysis began as a branch of neurological medicine which was deployed in relation to unexplained physical symptoms, and was subsequently used as a psychiatric therapy to treat emotional disturbances, it ended as a form of psychotherapy which was sometimes administered to 'analysands' who were not considered to be ill at all.

As Freud, who was always anxious to attract followers, gradually established psychoanalysis as an organised international movement, it became accepted that before any new disciple could practise as a psychoanalyst, he or she should first undergo analysis themselves. Although this convention only became established in the years after the First World War, many leading psychoanalysts submitted to being analysed, sometimes by Freud himself. Perhaps the most remarkable of all Freud's 'patients' was his own daughter, Anna.

Anna had gradually become Freud's most beloved child. He was attracted by her impish naughtiness and referred to her affectionately as his Black Devil. When she entered analysis in 1918 at the age of twenty-two it was purely because of her own wish to become a qualified lay psychoanalyst. Freud, however, was evidently concerned that he might, by this point in her life, have effaced her original vitality and demanded too much devotion from her. He therefore saw the analysis as an opportunity to help rescue her from 'excessive sublimation'. According to his own theories this would be achieved by freeing her from 'clitoral sexuality', and the auto-erotic activities deemed to be associated with it, into full 'genitality'.

When, in 1922, Anna Freud wrote her first psycho-analytic paper she gave an account of a girl who began to indulge in masochistic fantasies between the age of five and six. Her 'beating fantasy' was said to derive from an earlier incestuous fantasy involving her father. Each of the beating scenes ended by arousing the girl to masturbation. The girl is said to have succeeded in replacing these fantasies by a series of daydreams which she called her 'nice stories'. However, sometimes these failed to drive the old fantasies away and a pleasant daydream 'was suddenly replaced by the old beating situation together with the sexual gratification associated with it, which then led to a full discharge of the accumulated excitement'. Apparently the girl herself did not remember these occasions, since the paper records that 'such incidents were quickly forgotten, excluded from memory, and consequently treated as though they had not happened.'[33]

When Anna Freud read her paper to the Vienna Psycho-analytic Society in 1922 no clue was given to the identity of the analyst or the patient. Only after Anna Freud's death in 1982 was it publicly acknowledged that the analyst was Freud and the patient Anna herself. Her own paper made it quite clear that the mastubatory scenes at the heart of the analysis had been deduced by the analyst rather than related to him by the patient: 'Owing to her shame and resistance all she could ever be induced to give were short and covert allusions which left to the analyst the task of completing and reconstructing a picture of the original situation.'

From the records of the analysis which survive it is evident that, as in the case of Dora, Freud had concluded that the sexual development of his own daughter had been inhibited by childhood masturbation and that it was essential for the effectiveness of the treatment that these forgotten scenes should be recalled by her. On this occasion it would appear that his patient, who perhaps had no alternative, accepted his reconstructions.

If one of the conscious purposes of Freud's analysis of his daughter was to release her from excessive sublimation, then it appears to have failed. If anything the analysis seems to have deepened Anna's dependence on her father. She remained one of the most chastely devoted of all Freud's disciples and eventually became a distinguished psychoanalyst in her own right. When, having fled Vienna, Freud eventually died in London in 1939, it was to Anna that he entrusted his own 'frail child' – to use the term which he once applied to the psychoanalytic movement. In 1971, when a survey was conducted among American psychiatrists and psychoanalysts to establish whom they regarded as their most outstanding colleagues, Anna Freud was mentioned more often than anyone else. By this time psychoanalysis had become a movement which encircled the globe and Freud's status as one of the greatest thinkers of the twentieth century – and perhaps of any century – seemed to have been established almost beyond question.

FREUD AND CHARCOT

The psychoanalytic movement is undoubtedly a power-ful one which has endured one century and is likely to endure another. But from the very beginning Freud's theories have attracted criticism. This criticism has tended to become better informed with the passing of time. With almost a hundred years of Freud scholarship to draw on, it is now possible, perhaps for the first time, to offer a considered and balanced judgement on the value both of Freud's thought and of the movement he founded.

One of the obstacles which, perhaps more than any other, has stood in the way of a full understanding of Freud's ideas, is that many of those who have written about psychoanalysis, in Europe, in Britain or in America, have been scholars involved in the humanities. Whether writing as champions or critics, they have tended to present psychoanalysis as a humanistic discipline. As a result we often forget that it was in its origins a medical movement.

Psychoanalysis was born not, as is frequently claimed, out of the foibles of emotionally unstable middle-class women who came to consult Freud in Vienna. It was born amidst the florid and sometimes extreme physical symptoms displayed by patients who had been consigned to one of France's greatest hospitals – La Salpêtrière in Paris. The original begetter of the theory of unconscious symptom-formation – a theory which lies at the heart of psychoanalysis – was not Freud, nor even Breuer, but Jean-Martin Charcot.

Charcot was not a psychologist, he was a neurologist. His greatest gift was a genius for anatomical dissection and post-mortem diagnosis. His greatest handicap was that he practised neurology at a time when techniques of tissue-staining were primitive, X-rays had not been discovered and the instruments of investigation which have made modern neuroscience possible did not exist. The electroencephalogram (EEG), which would revolutionise neurology and psychiatry, was not in general use until the 1940s. Other techniques for brain-imaging, such as Magnetic Resonance Imaging (MRI), were not introduced until the closing decades of the twentieth century. Even today, at the beginning of the twenty-first century, the process of charting the brain's intricate functioning has barely begun. As Rita Carter writes in her book *Mapping the Mind*, 'the vision of the brain we have now is probably no more complete or accurate than a sixteenth-century map of the world.'[34]

In 1886, at the time of Freud's crucial encounter with Charcot, the map was scarcely drawn at all. Neurologists inhabited a world of almost complete diagnostic darkness, illuminated only by the occasional gleam of medical insight. Perhaps more importantly still, leading neurologists remained blissfully unaware of the depth of their ignorance. Charcot himself believed that the work of neurology was almost complete.

What this meant in practice was that many subtle neurological disorders, such as temporal lobe epilepsy, and frontal lobe epilepsy, were unrecognised in Charcot's day. At the same time, the *internal* pathology of head injuries remained an almost complete mystery. Closed head injuries, which produce concussion without leaving any external injury, were simply not recognised. This was the diagnostic darkness within which the fundamental principles of psychoanalysis were formulated. The medical and intellectual consequences are perhaps best illustrated by Charcot's classic case of traumatic hysteria – a case involving a patient known as 'Le Log——'.

Le Log—— was a florist's delivery man in Paris. One evening in October 1885, he was wheeling his barrow home through busy streets when it was hit from the side by a carriage which was being driven at great speed. Le Log——, who had been holding the handles of his barrow tightly, was spun through the air and landed on the ground. He was picked up completely unconscious. He was then taken to the nearby Beaujon hospital where he remained unconscious for five or six days. Six months later he was transferred to La Salpêtrière. By this time the lower extremities of his body were almost completely paralysed, there was a twitching or tremor in the corner of his mouth, he had a permanent headache and there were 'blank spaces in the tablet of his memory'. In particular he could not remember the accident itself. But, because there had never been any signs of external injury, Charcot decided that Le Log—— was a victim of traumatic hysteria and that his symptoms had arisen as a result of the psychological trauma he had suffered. Charcot came to this conclusion knowing full well that some weeks after his accident Le Log—— had suffered heavy nose-bleeds and a series of violent seizures – seizures which Charcot deemed hysterical.

In the century which has passed since Charcot made this diagnosis, the face of neurology – and of general medicine – has been transformed. If Le Log—— were to be brought today to a hospital in practically any part of the Western world there can be no doubt that doctors would recognise a case of closed head injury complicated by late epilepsy and raised intracranial pressure.

From this we may derive a conclusion which is both simple and terrible in its implications: Le Log——, the classic example of a patient who supposedly suffered from traumatic hysteria, did not forget because he was frightened. He forgot because he was concussed. His various symptoms were not produced by an unconscious idea. They were the result of brain damage.

We are here confronted by what may well be the most momentous medical misunderstanding which has taken place in the last two centuries. For Charcot's failure to recognise cases of closed head injury, and the symptoms they gave rise to, would shape the development of psychoanalysis. It was the main factor which would eventually lead Freud to elaborate his entire theory of unconscious symptom-formation – or 'repression'.

MORE MEDICAL MISTAKES

Charcot's misdiagnosis of Le Log—— (and of other victims of similar accidents) was not an isolated medical misunderstanding. It was but one part of a vast labyrinth of medical error which had been created over hundreds of years, and which Charcot himself had brought to an unprecedented level of complexity. In conditions where hundreds of subtle neurological disorders and other medical conditions remained wholly or largely unrecognised, the failure to make accurate medical diagnoses had led, almost inevitably, to the massive inflation of a pseudo-diagnosis – 'hysteria'.

When Charcot was confronted by patients who adopted the *arc-de-cercle* position by compulsively arching themselves backwards, he was not to know that this posture (which is sometimes combined with rhythmic pelvic thrusting) was a characteristic manifestation of frontal lobe epilepsy. In fact this form of epilepsy would not be fully described until another hundred years had passed. Even temporal lobe epilepsy, with its bizarre hysterical-seeming symptoms, was not recognised until the 1930s or 1940s. Confronted by the symptoms of these medically uncharted conditions, Charcot had little option but to place them in the catch-all diagnostic category of an illness – 'hysteria' – for whose existence no reliable clinical evidence has ever been produced.

What made the resulting labyrinth of medical error all but inescapable was that practically every other physician had become lost within it. Over and over again, highly trained medical practitioners, confronted by some of the more subtle symptoms of epilepsy, head injury, cerebral tumours, multiple sclerosis, Parkinson's disease, Tourette's syndrome, autism, syphilis, encephalitis, torsion dystonia, viral hepatitis, reflux oesophagitis, hiatus hernia and hundreds of other common or uncommon conditions, would resolve their diagnostic uncertainty by enlarging the category of hysteria yet further. As a result medical misconceptions which sprang from one misdiagnosis would almost inevitably receive support, and apparent confirmation, from misdiagnoses made by other physicians.

Just such a process of spectral 'corroboration' through multiple misdiagnosis lies at the heart of the development of psychoanalysis. For when Freud prevailed upon Breuer to publish an account of the case of Anna O., Charcot's own medical misjudgements were compounded in a manner which would have lasting consequences. In the closing years of the nineteenth century it was almost inevitable that Breuer should have construed Anna O.'s bizarre-seeming, apparently unrelated symptoms, as 'hysteria'. At the beginning of the twenty-first century, however, it is clear that each of Anna O.'s most significant symptoms corresponds to a specific kind of brain lesion or a recognisable pattern of brain pathology. More importantly still, many of these symptoms are typical components of complex partial seizures – which is to say a particular form of temporal lobe epilepsy.

Characteristic manifestations of such seizures include blurred vision, double-vision, feelings of de-personalisation, prosopagnosia (the inability to recognise faces), visual illusions which include the misidentification of objects, distortions in which upright objects appear tilted, or the walls of a room appear to bend. All of these symptoms Anna O. had. Not only this but the apparently unrelated dysfunctions which Breuer describes suggest a particular pattern of brain pathology. Anna O.'s problem with speech, for example, resembles the language deficit known as 'non-fluent aphasia'. This is caused by a lesion in the lauguage-area of the brain (Broca's area) on the left side of the frontal lobe. Because such lesions generally involve the adjacent motor cortex, most patients also suffer from a partial paralysis of the right side of the body, which is usually greater in the arm. In other words the conjunction of Anna O.'s disturbances of language with the paralysis which affected her right extremities, far from suggesting 'hysteria', indicates diffuse damage to a particular region of the brain. The underlying medical condition which gave rise to such brain pathology is likely to remain for ever unknown. But the neurological basis of Anna O.'s illness, though still disputed by some, has by now been placed beyond reasonable doubt.[35]

If this were the only misdiagnosis ever to have played a role in the development of psychoanalysis it would be momentous, since it led to the very creation of the technique. When Freud himself attempted to apply this technique to his own patients, however, he left behind him a trail of similar misdiagnoses.

Freud's first patient, Frau Emmy von N., was, as we have seen, afflicted by convulsive movements of her face and neck and the compulsion to shout out and make clicking sounds. Just such movements of the muscles of the face and neck, coupled with involuntary utterances, are classic signs of Tourette's syndrome. Today Frau Emmy would almost certainly be diagnosed as suffering from a variant of this neurological disorder.

Lucy R., the English governess who experienced hallucinations centring on the smell of burnt pudding, was another of Freud's patients whose symptoms would now be seen as having a neurological origin. Recurrent olfactory hallucinations are frequently found in temporal lobe epilepsy; the neurologist Doris Trauner, for example, writes that 'Some patients complain of intense olfactory hallucinations that in most cases are unpleasant (e.g. a smell of rotten eggs or burnt toast).'[36] In the case of Elisabeth von R., Freud himself admitted that the pain she experienced in her legs was 'rheumatic in origin' but claimed (implausibly) that it had been taken over by hysteria as 'a mnemic symbol of her painful psychical excitations'.[37] In yet another case, that of Dora, Freud knew that doctors had diagnosed appendicitis and that this was accompanied by a dragging of the right foot. He confidently repudiated this

45

diagnosis, claiming that Dora's abdominal pains were the throes of a hysterical childbirth, and that her dragging foot indicated her knowledge that she had made 'a false step'. Two surgeons, however, have since pointed out that a dragging foot could be caused by *pelvic* appendicitis, and that pain in the right leg is even used as a diagnostic test for this condition.[38]

If there should be any residual doubt about whether Freud's ideas about hysteria led him to make serious diagnostic errors, it is dispelled by Freud himself. In 1901 he described an occasion when a fourteen-year-old girl had fallen ill 'of an unmistakable hysteria'. Freud claimed that the hysteria 'cleared up' under his care. However, the girl still complained of the abdominal pains 'which had played the chief part in the clinical picture of hysteria'. Two months later she died of sarcoma of the abdominal glands. Although Freud sought to mitigate his error by claiming that hysteria had used the tumour as 'a provoking cause', there could not conceivably have been any evidence to support this view.[39]

DID FREUD CURE HIS PATIENTS?

If Freud's early patients were, for the most part, not suffering from psychological disturbances at all, and if Freud's therapeutic technique was founded on the medical errors of Charcot, it might well be asked how it was that he (and Breuer) succeeded in curing so many patients in the remarkable fashion attested to by the early case histories.

The first patient whose cure by psychoanalysis was proclaimed to the world was, of course, Anna O. In his account of the case Breuer quite clearly described how, after a climactic session in which Anna O. had recalled a frightening hallucination, 'the whole illness was brought to a close.' The story of her dramatic cure promptly became the founding miracle of psychoanalysis. In fact, however, no such cure ever took place. A year after Breuer had broken off his treatment of Anna O., he had confided to Freud that the patient he had supposedly cured 'was quite unhinged and that he wished she would die and so be released from her suffering'. Anna O. did subsequently improve, but a few years later, after a long stay in a sanatorium, she was still suffering from hallucinatory states in the evening.

The manner in which Freud dealt with this knowledge is perhaps best understood by reference to another case in which he became involved. In 1885, while researching the effects of cocaine, he persuaded a colleague, Ernst von Fleischl-Marxow, to take the drug in order to wean him from an addiction to morphine. Although Freud publicly reported that his colleague had been cured and that 'no cocaine habituation set in', Fleischl-Marxow had in fact become severely addicted to cocaine and had been reduced to a state of physical and mental wretchedness.

Just as, in 1885, Freud had reported the treatment of his colleague as having been successful, so, ten years later, he endorsed Breuer's published case history, even though he knew that Breuer's claim to have cured Anna O. was false.

In recounting his own psychoanalytic cases Freud frequently gave an assessment of his therapeutic role which was misleading in a similar way.

When he described the outcome of his treatment of Emmy von N. he equivocated, attempting to claim some therapeutic credit even though it is clear that her illness was not cured. In the case of Elisabeth von R. he was obliged to admit that her lameness had returned after the completion of the treatment. He then gave his case history a fairy-tale ending when he claimed (improbably) that he had managed to obtain an invitation to a private ball she was attending and was able to observe his former patient, six months after the treatment ended, 'whirl past in a lively dance'. Freud's own implicit estimation of his role in this alleged cure was not shared by his patient. Years later, talking to her daughter, she described Freud as 'just a young, bearded nerve specialist they sent me to'. He had tried 'to persuade me that I was in love with my brother-in-law, but that wasn't really so'.[40]

Once again it is Freud himself who dispels any doubts there may be about his habit of presenting as cures or partial cures, courses of treatment which had in fact been unsuccessful. For it is clear from his own subsequent statements (and above all from his private admissions to Fliess) that, when he claimed publicly that he had tested his seduction theory successfully on eighteen patients and implied that some of these had been cured, he was not telling the truth. The real situation, as he would eventually confide in Fliess, was that he had not succeeded in curing a

48

single patient, and there was no clinical evidence that his theory had any merit whatsoever.

RECONSTRUCTING MEMORIES

A further implication of the medical mistakes on which psychoanalysis was founded is that the particular process of unconscious symptom-formation ('repression'), invoked by Freud in order to account for physical symptoms, was an illusion. There is therefore no reason to suppose that the traumatic incidents which Freud purported to uncover had any pathogenic power or, indeed, that they ever took place.

Freud himself once acknowledged, in relation to the seduction theory, that he was 'prepared to let my belief run ahead of the evidential force of the observations I have made so far'.[41] This was an understatement. One of the reasons that the data of psychoanalysis sometimes appears to be so persuasive is that Freud, enraptured by his theories, had devised a method which, to a considerable extent, allowed him to create his own data. Instead of theories being based on observations, 'observations' were sometimes derived from theories.

This inversion of normal scientific procedure is not always immediately visible in Freud's case histories because he often presents the primal scenes or traumatic incidents which allegedly gave rise to his patients' symptoms as genuine and spontaneous memories imparted by the patient. In most cases, however, they are Freud's own constructions, born out of his own theoretical imagination. It is only after they have been created in this manner that Freud, by using the ingenious and infinitely flexible strategies of interpretation which he himself had created, reasons backwards in order to create a series of artificial links through which he contrives to derive them from his patients' dreams, associations or recollections.

The classic example of Freud's technique of reconstruction is provided by the case of the Wolf Man. The primal scene which Freud describes, according to which his parents woke him from his slumbers by repeatedly having sexual intercourse in front of him, clearly has its origins in Freud's theoretical preconceptions. It bears no discernible relationship to the dream from which Freud purports to derive it, and the links and interpretations by which he claims to do so are forced and implausible. It may be noted, indeed, that this particular reconstruction has stretched beyond breaking-point the credulity even of some of Freud's followers. As the psychoanalyst Erich Fromm has written: 'To form a hypothesis about what actually happened when the boy was one-and-a-half from a dream which says nothing more than that the boy saw some wolves, seems to be an example of obsessional thinking with complete disregard for reality.'[42] Even Fromm's judgement is too generous, however. For, although the primal scene is indeed a hypothesis, the crucial factor is that Freud himself treats it as though it were an established fact and makes it into the keystone of the entire analysis.

When Freud builds on this foundation by claiming that,

at a late stage of the analysis, 'there emerged timidly and indistinctly, a kind of recollection that at a very early age ... [the patient] must have had a nursery-maid who was very fond of him', his very language gives rise to suspicion, as does his claim that the case was now rapidly resolved. When interviewed at the age of eighty-three about his time in analysis, Freud's former patient recalled many details lucidly and clearly. But he could recall no miraculous transformation of his condition. More importantly, although he knew that Grusha was supposed to be a nursery maid, he could not remember her at all. There can be little doubt that the Grusha scene was another of Freud's constructions. In this case, however, it seems possible that Freud had actually fabricated the scene after the event and then interpolated it into his case history as the 'solution' to what would otherwise have remained a therapeutic riddle.[43]

In the case of the Wolf Man's dream it seems to be beyond question that Freud did not succeed in reconstructing a repressed *memory*. He succeeded only in constructing a hypothetical memory which he then tried to persuade his patient to accept. In doing this Freud was effectively repeating the errors he had made in his 'seduction theory'. For it was in relation to this theory that he himself eventually conceded that the scenes he constructed for his patients had not been genuine memories at all.

If we are to understand the development of psychoanalysis, it is essential to recognise that, when Freud renounced his seduction theory in 1897, he was not bravely abandoning a cherished theory because of the evidence, as some have claimed. Rather he was seeking to retain his theory of repression and the analytic methods associated with it *in spite* of the fact that they had repeatedly led to erroneous conclusions.

When he subsequently sought to persuade Dora that she had masturbated even though she had no recollection of doing so, when he successfully persuaded his daughter Anna that she had indulged in sado-masochistic daydreams whose details she had repressed, and when, by interpreting a dream, he sought to persuade the Wolf Man that, at the age of eighteen months, he had witnessed his parents copulating from behind three times in an afternoon, Freud was using the same analytic methods as he had done in 1896. The main difference was that, by generally refraining from reconstructing sexual *crimes* (which inevitably involved other people who might contest or disprove the reconstruction), and by focusing instead on events, impulses or ideas which were uncontroversial, private or unwitnessed, Freud ensured that his theory of repression could not be easily rebutted and became in practice unfalsifiable.

FREUD'S FLIESSIAN SCIENCE

Even Erich Fromm has recognised Freud's habit of effectively constructing 'facts'. He writes that the account of the Wolf Man's dream 'is actually a testimony to Freud's capacity and inclination to build up reality out of a hundred little incidents either surmised or gained by interpretation, torn out of context and used in the service of arriving at conclusions that fit his preconceived idea'.[44] One of the reasons that Fromm was able to retain some allegiance to Freud, in spite of this brutally accurate description of his methods, is that he was unaware of the labyrinth of medical error out of which psychoanalysis had emerged. Just as importantly, he was not acquainted with the biological origins of the theory of infantile sexuality. These, indeed, have remained invisible to most observers for almost a century.

The biological basis of Freud's theory of infantile sexuality, however, was no more secure than the medical origins of the theory of unconscious symptom-formation. For while it is evidently the case that the human embryo does recapitulate various stages of evolutionary development, the specific 'psychobiological' claims made by Fliess, Haeckel, Bölsche and others about sexual development were pure speculation.

It is quite true that the role which is sometimes played by the mouth and the anus in human sexual behaviour is remarkable in that it usually has no reproductive function. However, there is no reason to suppose, as Freud implies, that homosexuals are fixated at a particular stage of 'perverted' sexual development which corresponds phylogenetically to that reached by some of our pre-mammalian ancestors. Nor is there any evidence that sexual impulses are organised in relation to particular anatomical zones, or that they pass through any predetermined developmental sequence resembling that described by Freud.

Even if we were to accept, as Freud claims, that sucking is

intrinsically sexual, then it would appear that this form of satisfaction is not extinguished by genital sexuality but continues, finding expression in the pleasures of kissing, fellatio and cunnilingus. Although moralists might categorise such activities as perversions, biology, *pace* Freud, affords no reason for doing so. Similarly, while it may be the case that the mucous membrane of the anus gives rise to pleasurable sensations when stimulated, there is no evidence to suggest that such sensitivity diminishes or disappears with sexual maturity. Those who, whether in the context of heterosexual or homosexual relationships, some-times practise anal intecourse, are availing themselves of a kind of sensitivity which endures naturally and normally in all human beings. The suggestion that they are fixated at some primitive level of development or that they are biologically debarred from the pleasures of genital sexual-ity, is one for which there is no scientific evidence.

Once again we find that, rather than moving from observations to theories, Freud has begun with a theory and has then reasoned backwards and marshalled a series of 'observations' which are then falsely presented as the data from which the theory was derived. To cite but one example, Freud argues that children are induced to forgo the sexual pleasure associated with the anus and excretion by being told 'that everything that has to do with these functions is improper and must be kept secret'. This argument, if closely examined, is clearly specious. On the one hand, if there was indeed a biological sequence of development which led to the relinquishing of the early erotogenic zones, as Freud postulates, there would be no need of the cultural sanctions he invokes. At the same time it is clear that the kinds of taboo described by Freud are applied to 'ordinary' sexuality as well. Yet it would never be suggested that such taboos lead children (or adults) to forgo genital sexual pleasure. Indeed, if anything, secrecy and taboo heighten sexual excitement rather than lessen it.

Both the real status of the 'explanations' which are offered by the theory of infantile sexuality, and the manner in which Freud reasons backwards from theory to 'data', are best illustrated if, in addition to the three stages of sexual development described by Freud, we postulate the existence of a fourth stage. This new stage of psychosexual development, which relates to the erotogenic significance of the hands, and intervenes between the oral and anal stages, would be known as the 'manual stage'. This concept would immediately explain aspects of the Oedipal tie between the mother and child which are often neglected, and in particular the compulsive hand-holding so frequently indulged in by mothers and children in our culture.

As well as accounting for the importance of manual fondling during sexual foreplay, it would also explain such perverse practices as digital stimulation of the anus during love-making, which evidently results from a fixation at the two earliest stages of sexual development. It would also illuminate the role played by the hand in auto-erotic practices and would thus extend Freud's own observation, made initially in relation to the mouth and the anus, that 'certain regions of the body . . . seem, as it were, to be claiming that they should themselves be regarded and treated as genitals.'[45]

The newly defined manual stage would be especially useful in therapy, and would help to illuminate the aetiology of the 'manual character'. This character-type is found in two forms, both showing infantile traits. In the manual-erotic personality we find a series of character-traits in which an excessive generosity or *open-handedness* is found in association with compulsive, dependent or *clinging* behaviour, together with an over-readiness to submit to authority. In the manual-sadistic personality this character syndrome is found in an inverted form as a consequence of reaction-formations; hence meanness – *tight-fistedness* – will be found in association with officiousness – the desire to *manipulate* others.

The problem with Freud's fiction of oral and anal erotism is that it has functioned as just the kind of elastic, catch-all hypothesis which is exemplified by my own fiction of manual erotism. Although his scheme of development originally played only a limited role, he gradually extended it in a series of papers on character-development, until practically any form of human behaviour could be located within it.

The infinitely flexible nature of psychoanalytic explanations might well be compared to the flexible nature of an explanatory procedure which was both historically and personally close to psychoanalysis – that devised by Wilhelm Fliess. Fliess, it will be recalled, believed he could analyse the whole realm of biology by using the figures of 23 and 28, both of which he had derived from the duration of the menstrual cycle. Although the phenomenon of biological periodicity is a real one, the most level-headed assessment of Fliess's achievement is perhaps that made by the mathematician Martin Gardner, who has pointed out that Fliess's 'Teutonic crackpottery' depended on analysing all his data in terms of the general formula $x \cdot 23 \pm y \cdot 28$. Gardner observes that any two positive integers which, like 23 and 28, have no common denominator, can be used in this general formula to produce any positive number which is desired. Since Fliess's formula contained every possible answer, no problem of periodicity could, *a priori*, avoid falling victim to its explanatory power.[46]

The Fliessian character of Freud's explanatory hypotheses is perhaps best conveyed in a statement which Freud made about the way in which infantile 'instinct-components' supposedly determine the personalities of adult 'neurotics'. This will be found in Freud's paper of 1908, 'Character and Anal Erotism':

> We ... can lay down a formula for the way in which character in its final shape is formed out of the constituent instincts: the permanent character traits *are either unchanged prolongations of the original instincts, or sublimations of those instincts, or reaction formations against them* [italics added].[47]

If we place this 'formula' alongside Fliess's use of arithmetic, it is difficult to avoid concluding that, in the way he manipulated such concepts as 'anal-erotism' and 'oral-erotism', Freud succeeded in translating Fliess's numerological mysticism into a more subtle conceptual mysticism. For Freud could not only marry his concepts together into such combinations as oral-anal, or anal-sadistic, he could also subject them to quasi-arithmetical transformations and inversions by using such conceptual operators as 'reaction-formation', 'sublimation' and 'fixation'. Just as Fliess's periodic values of 28 and 23 led a double life, concealing behind their outward mathematical sobriety a bewildering promiscuity of application, so Freud's ostensibly stable concepts led a similar double life, and it was this which gave them the catch-all qualities I have tried to illustrate.

A similar observation might be made of Freud's techniques of dream interpretation, which depended on construing all dreams as cryptic forms of wish-fulfilment. As Fliess manipulated numbers, so Freud juggled with symbols until even the most frustrating or tragic dream could be interpreted as secretly fulfilling some wish or desire of the dreamer – usually, though not always, a sexual wish.

Freud thus argues that whenever steps, staircases and ladders appear in dreams, they are 'unquestionably' symbols of copulation:

It is hard not to discover the basis of the comparison: we come to the top in a series of rhythmical movements and with increasing breathlessness, and then, with a few rapid leaps, we can get to the bottom again. Thus the rhythmical pattern of copulation is reproduced in going upstairs.[48]

The fact that this argument could be applied to practically any form of rhythmical muscular exercise, from paddling a canoe to polishing a floor, is ignored. When Freud goes on to write that women's hats 'can very often be interpreted with certainty as a genital organ (usually a man's)', that the same is true of overcoats and ties, and that not only tools and weapons but all forms of luggage and some kinds of relatives (particularly sons, daughters and sisters) frequently symbolise genitals, as do noses, eyes, ears and mouths, it is difficult not to suspect a kinship between Freud's interpretive strategies and Fliess's arithmetic.

FREUD'S LEGACY

It would appear that one of the reasons Freud fell under the influence, firstly of Charcot's medical misapprehensions, and then of the wildly speculative theorising of his friend Fliess, was that the ideas they advanced both seemed to meet his need for a world-redeeming revelation. So great was Freud's anxiety to receive such a revelation that he appears to have been unable to interrogate sceptically any speculative construction which held out the promise of supplying it.

Yet although Freud's relationship to knowledge resembled that of the messianic prophet or mystic, he himself triumphantly claimed the title of 'scientist'. Psychoanalysis, he wrote, 'has put us in a position to establish psychology on foundations similar to those of any other science, such, for instance, as physics'.[49] Freud's belief that he was constructing a genuine science remains crucial to any understanding of how psychoanalysis developed. For it was his relentless and reductive scientism which, coupled with his compulsive need for fame, led him deeper and deeper into a labyrinth of error.

It is quite true that Freud pointed to the poets as the precursors of psychoanalysis. But the whole point of this claim was to suggest that psychoanalysis had succeeded in translating 'poetic' insights into human nature into a 'hard' scientific register. In practice such insights were incorporated into psychoanalysis only after they had been both technicalised and medicalised. Again and again Freud strangled in false science the very poetic truths he had glimpsed in imaginative literature. When it comes to psychological insight, the common wealth of our literary tradition remains richer by far than psychoanalysis, and this should be recognised more widely than it is.

Yet, partly because of the way in which he used the aura of science and medicine to gain intellectual authority for his theories, Freud sometimes seems to be regarded as the only possible source for any deep insight into human nature. Although the idea that human motives are often unconscious is an ancient one, Freud is persistently credited with this 'discovery'. Psychoanalysis, indeed, has become a kind of dead letter box into which any profound insight into human nature whose origins are obscure, unknown or insufficiently 'scientific', is automatically sorted. At the same time the formulations which have sometimes been made by Freud's followers, some of whom possess a degree of genuine psychological insight, have been used to enrich the image of the master. As a result we tend to hide the real, historical Freud behind a mythical figure who rules over an empire of almost infinite psychological depth and complexity. The reality, as should by now be apparent, was very different. It is not simply that Freud lacked the extraordinary psychological insight he has been credited with. It is that, both in his theoretical formulations and in his case histories, he frequently manifests a complete lack of *ordinary* psychological insight.

The question which remains, which is perhaps the most important of all, is why, as a culture, we have bestowed upon Freud the towering pre-eminence noted at the outset of this essay. One way of answering this question is to recall that, for centuries before the advent of psychoanalysis, psychology had focused almost entirely on the rational soul. It had not only ignored the animal body of human beings and their sexual impulses but, in the Platonic and Christian traditions, had actively denigrated these, representing them as belonging to a dark and demonic world or to the realm of sin and evil. It was, indeed, by constantly vitalising people's anxieties about their darker impulses that preachers and religious leaders traditionally sought to establish the need for redemption, while simultaneously looking forward to the apocalyptic moment when the Beast would be vanquished and the Chosen would be granted final dominion with God over the World, the Flesh and the Devil.

By promising fearlessly to explore and explain a realm which had hitherto been defined as evil, Freud was able to present himself to his followers, and to the world at large, as a revolutionary thinker. One of the most remarkable aspects of the 'science' which resulted, however, was that

Freud retained the religious concept of 'evil' and frequently had recourse to it. He wrote that the impulses which are subjected to repression *'can be summed up in general as evil'*. As we have seen, he described psychoanalysis itself as a process of conjuring up 'evil' demons. The Unconscious, he said elsewhere, is the place 'in which *all that is evil in the human mind is contained as a predisposition'*.[50]

Rooted as he was in the rationalism of the Judaeo-Christian tradition, which has always upheld the supremacy and the divine origin of reason, Freud remained passionately committed to a secularised version of the same rationalism. 'We have no other means of controlling our instinctual nature but our intelligence,' he wrote; '. . . the psychological ideal [is] the primacy of the intelligence.' 'Our mind,' he observed, '. . . is no peacefully self-contained unity. It is rather to be compared with a modern State in which a mob, eager for enjoyment and destruction, has to be held down forcibly by a prudent superior class.'[51]

When, in 1923, Freud revised his theory of personality by adding to it his tripartite division of the mind into 'id', 'ego' and 'superego', the undoubted appeal of these hypothetical entities arose directly from concepts which were already well established. In practice Freud was doing little more than reformulating in technical terms the idea that the human self is wrought out of a conflict between the conscience and unbridled instincts. Indeed, Freud himself was obliged to recognise the objection which was most commonly made against his ego psychology – that it 'comes down to nothing more than taking commonly used abstractions literally, and in a crude sense, and transforming them from concepts to things'.[52]

In the manner that he endorsed the supremacy of the conscience, as in other respects, Freud remained a profoundly traditional thinker. It is no accident that he identified with Moses, had 'a special sympathy' for St Paul, referred to himself as a 'fisher of men' and was sometimes compared by his followers to Jesus. 'I was the apostle of Freud who was my Christ!' recalled Wilhelm Stekel.[53]

There can be no doubt that, such religious comparisons notwithstanding, Freud genuinely believed that he was using science to sweep away superstition and introduce a new view of human nature. His real achievement in creating psychoanalysis, however, was to hide superstition beneath the rhetoric of reason in order to reintroduce a very old view of human nature. By portraying the unconscious or the 'id' as a seething mass of unclean instincts, and seeing men and women as driven by dark sexual and sadistic impulses and a secret love of excrement, Freud in effect reinvented, for a modern scientific age, the traditional Christian doctrine of Original Sin. At the same time, through psychoanalysis, he offered to all who followed him a means of redemption.

If, in the twentieth century, psychoanalysis rapidly attained the status and power of an orthodoxy, it was for no other reason than that it was a form of orthodoxy itself – a subtle reformulation of Judaeo-Christian doctrine in secular form, safe from the attacks of science precisely because it was presented *as* science.

The redemptive promise of psychoanalysis, however, has

proved to be an empty one. Today we remain just as much in thrall to our irrational impulses as we ever have been, and just as prone to demonising others by attributing to them the violent, sadistic or sexual impulses we are unwilling to acknowledge as our own. Far from releasing us from this predicament, psychoanalysis has, by promoting the illusion that our deepest sexual impulses and fantasies have already been analysed and rationally understood, made it even more acute. Psychoanalysis has not only failed to redeem us from such social ills; it has failed to do the only thing we ultimately have a right to demand of explanatory theories – it has failed to explain.

We should by no means assume from the failure of psychoanalysis that our sexual behaviour, or indeed any other aspect of our nature, is likely to remain forever veiled in mystery, or that it is not susceptible to human understanding. There is good reason to suggest, however, that an essential step towards such understanding is to recognise the labyrinth of medical error out of which Freud's intellectual system grew, and the false logic through which it was developed. For it is perhaps only by acknowledging both the complexity and the folly of one of the most significant of all attempts to understand our nature that we will render future attempts more likely to succeed.

SOURCES

In writing this essay I have drawn freely on my own earlier work, *Why Freud Was Wrong: Sin, Science and Psychoanalysis*, revised paperback edition, HarperCollins, 1996 (abbreviated as WFWW). Other references are to: *The Standard Edition of the Complete Psychological Works of Sigmund Freud*, ed. James Strachey, Hogarth Press and the Institute of Psychoanalysis, 24 volumes, 1953–74 (abbreviated as SE); *The Penguin Freud Library*, ed. Angela Richards and Albert Dickson, Penguin, 15 volumes, 1973–86 (abbreviated as PF); *The Complete Letters of Sigmund Freud to Wilhelm Fliess 1887–1904*, ed. Jeffrey Mousaieff Masson, Harvard University Press, 1985 (abbreviated as FF); Frank Cioffi, *Freud and the Question of Pseudoscience*, Open Court, Chicago, 1998; Allen Esterson, *Seductive Mirage: An Exploration of the Work of Sigmund Freud*, Open Court, Chicago, 1993; Erich Fromm, *Greatness and Limitations of Freud's Thought*, Jonathan Cape, 1980.

For more on Freud, psychoanalysis and related topics, go to www.richardwebster.net

1. Cioffi, p. 171.

2. SE11, pp. 9–20.

3. SE2, p. 154; PF3, p. 223.

4. SE2, p. 295; PF3, p. 282.

5. SE2, p. 6; PF3, p. 57.

6. SE1, p. 51.

7. FF, p. 25.

8. FF, p. 144.

9. SE3, p. 204.

10. SE3, pp. 195–6.

11. FF, p. 220.

12. FF, p. 226.

13. SE3, p. 199.

14. FF, p. 266.

15. WFWW, p. 222.

16. WFWW, p. 226; FF, p. 254.

17. WFWW, p. 230.

18. PF1, p. 356.

19. PF1, p. 357.

20. SE7, p. 241; PF7, pp. 166–7.

21. SE16, p. 354; PF1, p. 400.

22. FF, p. 268.

23. FF, p. 272.

24. SE23, p. 189; PF15, pp. 423–4.

25. SE23, p. 193; PF15, p. 428.

26. SE16, p. 337.

27. SE20, p. 34; PF15, pp. 217–19.

28. PF8, p. 93.

29. SE7, pp. 76–8; PF8, pp. 112–14.

30. PF8, p. 150.

31. PF9, p. 332.

32. PF9, p. 238.

33. WFWW, p. 411.

34. *Mapping the Mind*, Rita Carter, Weidenfeld, 1998, p. 4.

35. WFWW, pp. 112–35; p. xvi.

36. WFWW, p. 159.

37. SE2, p. 165; PF3, p. 237.

38. PF8, p. 143; WFWW, p. 198 (note).

39. SE6, p. 146 (note); PF5, pp. 197–8 (note).

40. WFWW, p. 164.

41. SE3, p. 200.

42. Fromm, p. 19.

43. Esterson, pp. 77–93.

44. Fromm, p. 19.

45. SE7, pp. 152–3; PF7, p. 65.

46. WFWW, p. 222.

47. SE9, p. 175; PF7, p. 215.

48. SE5, p. 355; PF4, p. 472.

49. SE26, pp. 193–7.

50. See WFWW, pp. 318–19.

51. SE21, p. 48; SE21, pp. 7–8.

52. SE19, p. 37.

53. WFWW, p. 305.